JAZZ DUETS

ETUDES FOR PHRASING AND ARTICULATION

RICHARD LOWELL

BERKLEE PRESS

Editor in Chief: Jonathan Feist
Senior Vice President of Online Learning and Continuing Education/CEO of Berklee Online: Debbie Cavalier
Vice President of Enrollment Marketing and Management: Mike King
Vice President of Academic Strategy: Carin Nuernberg
Editorial Assistant: Brittany McCorriston

ISBN 978-0-87639-206-5

Berklee
Press

1140 Boylston Street
Boston, MA 02215-3693 USA
(617) 747-2146

Visit Berklee Press Online at
www.berkleepress.com

Berklee Online

Study music online at
online.berklee.edu

DISTRIBUTED BY

HAL•LEONARD®
7777 W. BLUEMOUND RD. P.O. BOX 13819
MILWAUKEE, WISCONSIN 53213

Visit Hal Leonard Online
www.halleonard.com

Berklee Press, a publishing activity of Berklee College of Music, is a not-for-profit educational publisher.
Available proceeds from the sales of our products are contributed to the scholarship funds of the college.

CONTENTS

PREFACE

The duets in this book should benefit you in a number of ways. Since they are written as two part counterpoint rather than soli, each line is just as important as the other. There is really no first or second part, and you should consider whichever melody you are playing as the first part. It now becomes important that you not only concentrate on the accuracy of your melody but are also aware of the other melody and how your part interacts with it. This should develop or enhance your ability to play with others.

There are instances where one melody is "passed" to the other, so the idea is to make this sound like one continuous melody, even though it is played by two players. In a soli setting, you are both playing the same rhythm, so keeping the time feel is relatively easy. With these duets, each player must focus on playing their melody with a good sense of time, so it creates an accurate musical event between the two lines. This should instill or reinforce a good sense of "inner" time.

Since each part is different, it may also have different articulation and dynamics, so special attention must be payed to each.

There are six distinct styles within this book of duets.

- swing/bop
- ballads
- jazz waltz
- double-time funk (in a 2 feel)
- 6/8
- samba in 2

Swing and bop are essentially the same feel and are played the same. The word "bop" refers to a specific period of jazz. There is no notation that defines exactly how to play eighth notes in a swing style, so you must try to imagine that four eighth notes are played as though you have two groups of eighth-note triplets with the first two in each set being tied. This will give you a very good feel for eighth notes in a swing style.

All of the remaining five styles will see the eighth notes played evenly. There are some occasions where the eighth notes in a jazz waltz are played as "swing" eighths, but that is not the case in this book of duets. All ballads should be played with even eighth notes, and all notes held to their full value.

The two articulations used in this book are the jazz staccato (ʌ) and the legato (—). It's extremely important that each quarter note or tied eighth has a specific articulation. The legato means notes are played smoothly and connected, not separated. You will see this in the first two bars of "Not a Blues." The jazz staccato is a short but "fat" note. Going back to the triplet feel for swing eighth notes, this attack must be thought of as an eighth-note triplet with the first two notes tied and the last note eliminated (i.e., two-thirds of a quarter note in duration).

The classical staccato marking (.) is too short for most swing/bebop music; however, it does work in some even eighth-notes styles, such as funk and some Latin styles. I don't use the classical staccato in most of these duets, but understanding the difference is important.

We can affix certain syllables to these three kinds of articulation. The legato would have the sound and duration of "Doo;" the classical staccato "Dit;" and the jazz staccato "Dot." So, imagine four quarter notes with alternate articulations of legato and jazz staccato. The resulting sound would be Doo-Dot Doo-Dot.

Name	Symbol	Syllable
Legato	—	Doo
Jazz Staccato	ʌ	Dot
Classical Staccato	.	Dit

1. Shake and Bake

This is phrased as all four-bar phrases. The parentheses around the notes are meant to be "swallowed." These notes are sometimes called "ghost notes." The idea is to make them sound almost as non-existent, yet still there. It's easier to do on a wind instrument than on a guitar, piano, or other stringed instrument. Try the best you can to give these notes much less emphasis.

For wind instruments, there are a number of ways to achieve this effect. For brass players, you can put your tongue between your lips to deaden the sound, and for reed players, just touch the reed with your tongue to do the same.

Guitar notation typically uses × noteheads instead of parentheses for ghost notes. To achieve this effect on guitar, release the pressure on the string with the fretting hand, thereby giving the note less emphasis.

Shake and Bake

Easy Swing ♩ = 144

2. Whole with Half

Be sure to treat the "and" of beat 4 in measure 4 as though it belongs to the next phrase. This is for both parts. This situation occurs many times in this duet. In measures 23 and 24, be careful to line up the "ands" of the beats. As always, observe the dynamics.

Whole with Half

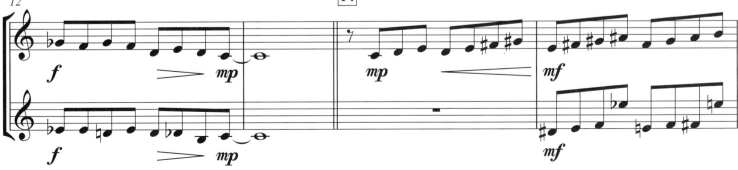

3. Bopularity

There is some odd phrasing in this duet. It starts with four-bar phrases right through
13, but starting at measure 9, it changes to two-bar phrases. The last bar before
13 includes "cross phrases," which means that the measure serves as not only an
end to the two-bar phrase but also acts as a pickup into 13. The section starting at
13 is unusual, as it is a three-bar phrase. You should recognize measure 27 as the
original motif in the very first bar of the duet. It is here that the last five-bar phrase
ends the piece.

Bopularity

Fast Bop ♩ = 200

4. A Familiar Face

As with all ballads, treat your individual line as a solo melody. Strive for a good sound, and hold each note to its full value. There is certainly nothing wrong with a touch of vibrato.

A Familiar Face

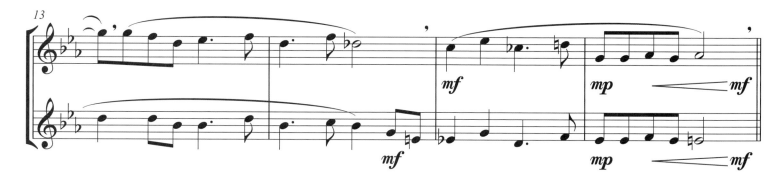

5. Spring?

Be very aware of the phrase markings through this piece, especially in the second part during the section beginning at **14**. They are usually grouped in threes, but watch out starting at measure 24 where the groupings are in sets of two.

Spring?

Jazz Waltz ♩ = 144

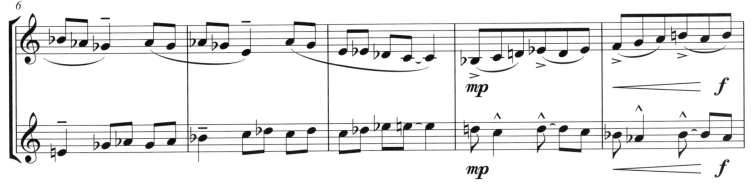

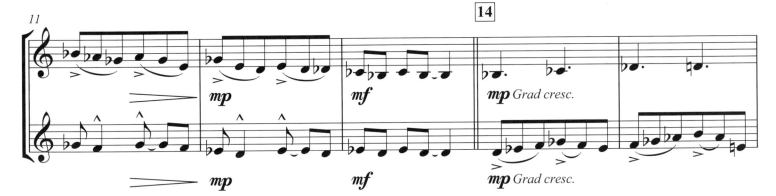

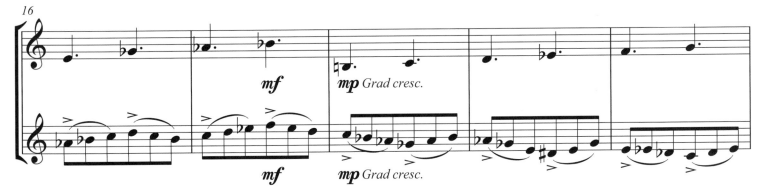

6. Flunk

This is a double-time funk feel, so be sure to count in 2. Even though you see dotted eighths and sixteenths in the bottom part, notice the articulations. Play these notes very short. The sixteenth notes should be played evenly, rather than swing. Most of the phrasing for this duet is in two-bar phrases.

Flunk

Double-Time Funk ♩ = 100

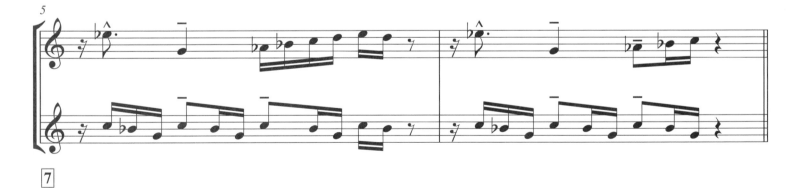

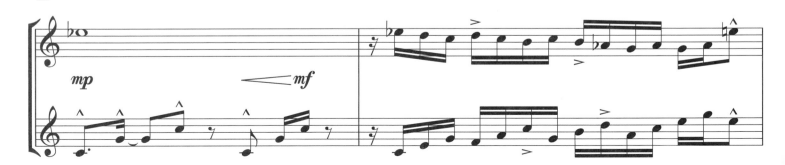

19

7. Big Skippy

This duet features some large intervals, so it is important to try to "hear" your note before you play it. This will develop a good sense of relative pitch. You are playing the note below and trying to hear the interval above or below. This "hearing" is important for intonation.

    Observe the two types of articulation in this duet. As discussed, the jazz staccato (∧) is played as though you have an eighth-note triplet with the first two notes tied and the last note eliminated. This will give you that nice "fat" percussive short note. The legato (–) should be played so that there is no space between the notes, every note is smoothly connected to the next.

Big Skippy

Easy Swing ♩ = 144

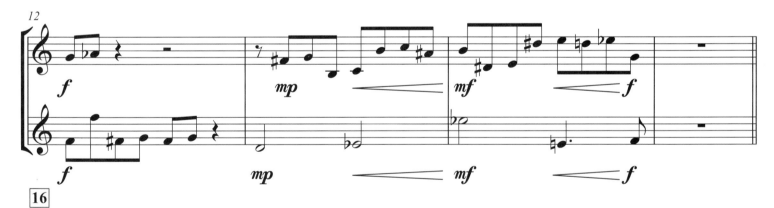

16

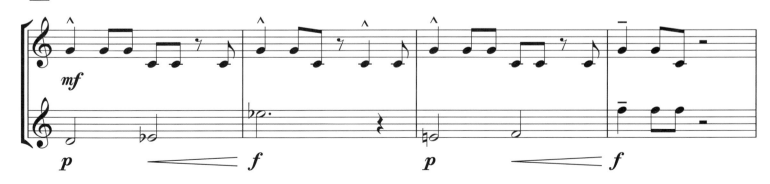

8. Luna Reflections

This is a ballad, and all of the phrase markings are provided. The eighth notes, as in all ballads, should be played evenly. Try to make sure everything is smooth and connected. Try not to rush the quarter-note triplets, as it is easy to do in a slow tempo. As with all these duets, each line is a melody all its own, so try to treat the part you are playing as a very important melody. This is especially true in a ballad.

Here, you should be working on your sound, and a hint of vibrato is encouraged.

Luna Reflections

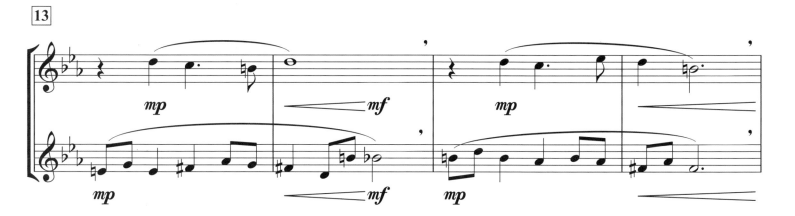

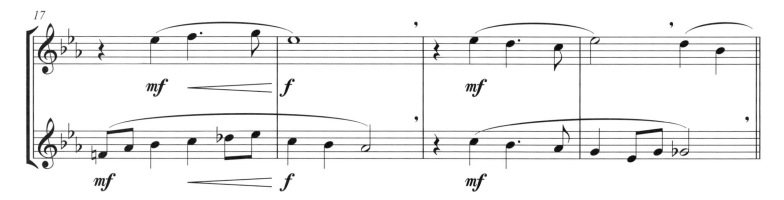

9. Par 3

This is a jazz waltz, so the eighth notes favor a more even eighth-note approach. Where you see accents ($>$), you should really emphasize those notes. Horn players use a strong tongue, supported by lots of air, to really "pop" them.

The duet starts with two-bar phrases and goes into four-bar phrases at rehearsal **9**. There is a slightly different feel in rehearsal **23**. Notice the phrase markings, as everything should be played smooth and connected. Rehearsal **45** remains with the same smooth and even feel, but we still have the accents in this section, so don't be afraid to exaggerate them.

Par 3

Jazz Waltz ♩ = 184

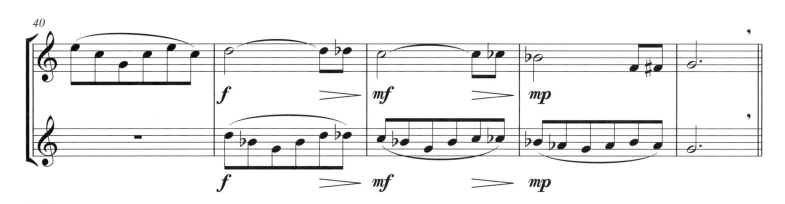

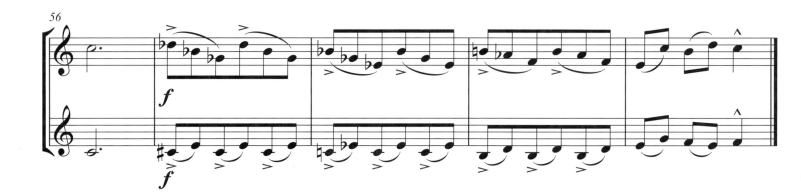

10. 6 + 8 = 14

In this piece, it is extremely important to emphasize both the accents and the phrase markings. Again, most of these phrase markings are in groups of three, but many are across the bar line, as you see in the second part, in measures 1 through 4. At **33**, we have that situation where we are passing the melody back and forth between the two parts. Also notice that the phrasing is between the parts. The second part has the accents on the second note of each set of three, so it is really important to emphasize those accents.

6 + 8 = 14

Evenly ♩. = 120

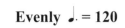

11. Triple Flip

It's easy to rush when playing triplets, and it's difficult to keep a good sense of time when going from eighth-note triplets to quarter-note triplets. Just be aware of this, and try to play relaxed through this triplet exercise.

Triple Flip

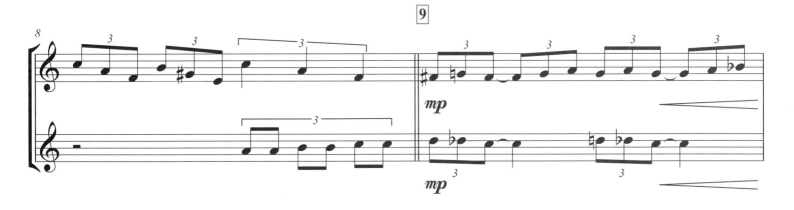

12. C Foam

This is a samba in 2, and so, another opportunity for you to practice counting and playing in 2. There are many places where the "and" of beat 4 belongs to the next phrase and should be played as such. Here are a few of those instances.

- In bar 3, the "and" of 4 belongs to the "and" of 1 in bar 4.
- In bar 7, the "and" of 4 belongs to the "and" of 1 in bar 8.
- We see the same thing in bar 9 and 10.

Although all are not marked, all of the tied eighth notes should be played long.

C Foam

Samba in 2 ♩ = 120

13. Fore

The phrasing in the beginning of this duet is four-bar phrases, changing to two-bar phrases at ⏹13. It then changes back to a four-bar phrase at the end of that section. We continue with four-bar phrases at ⏹23 until the end.

At measure 9, the melody in the top part becomes a bit angular and requires you to hear the notes involved in the large interval leaps.

In playing and listening, you will discover that the melody is made up of a series of perfect fourths, which should make hearing the intervals much easier. You will also see these series of perfect fourths in the top melody at measure 20.

Fore

13

14. Old BSOM

This should be played at a fast tempo, as the tempo marking indicates. This will make the eighth-note triplets difficult to play, so I suggest you begin at a slower tempo and work up to ♩ = 200. Start practicing this at 25 , and play this slower till the end. It is here where you will find the eighth-note triplets. Once you have worked 25 up to tempo, you're now ready to perform this from the beginning. NOTE: In measures 35–36, the alignment of the eighth-note triplets is difficult, so practice those bars slowly, and then increase them up to tempo.

Old BSOM

15. Green Leapers

Lots of big intervals here, so do your best to hear the note you are leaping into.
Measures 16–18 are rhythmically tricky, so concentrate on not rushing your line,
and align it properly with the other line.

Green Leapers

Easy Swing ♩ = 144

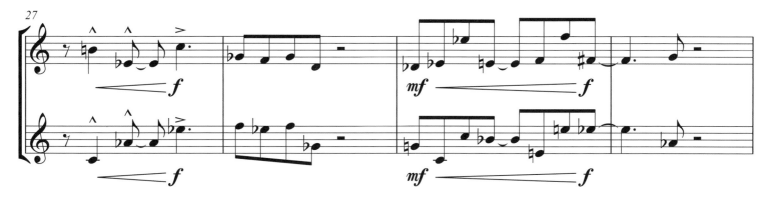

16. Carumba

This 6/8 piece should be played as you would a classical piece, with the eighth notes played very staccato—the classical staccato, not the jazz staccato. This may be one of the more difficult pieces to play with a good time feel. Once again, a strong 2 feel and very crisp "clipped" short notes.

Carumba

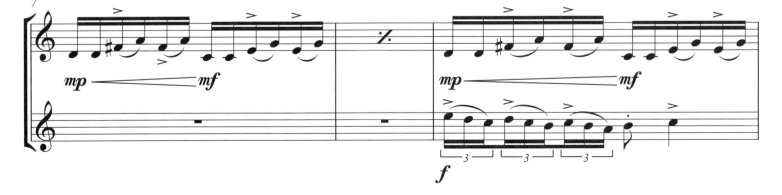

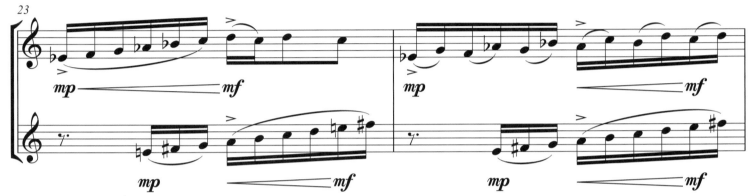

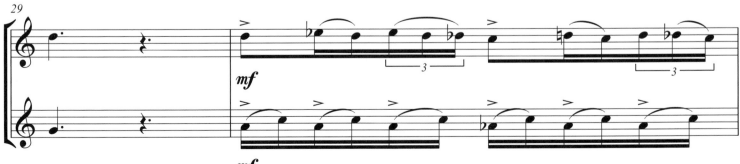

42

17. Thoughts of You

Here is another ballad where the eighth notes should be played evenly. Once again, all of the phrase markings have been provided. The focus on this, and all ballads, should be your individual sound and making sure you hold all notes to their full value. Slower tempos do have a tendency to rush, so focus on a relaxed time feel.

Thoughts of You

Grad. cresc.

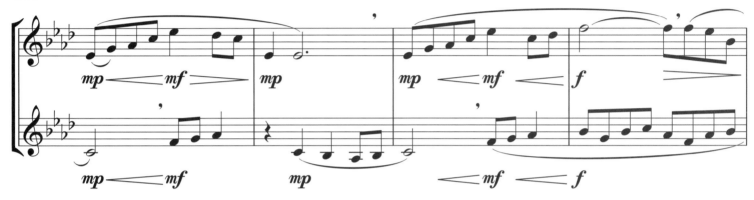

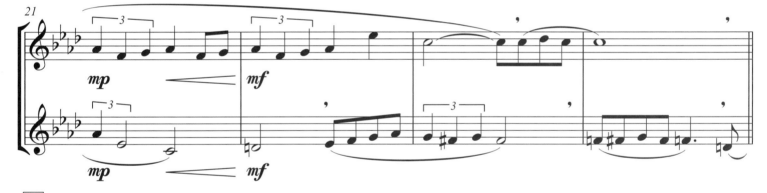

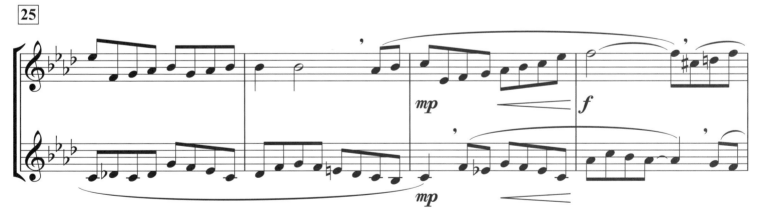

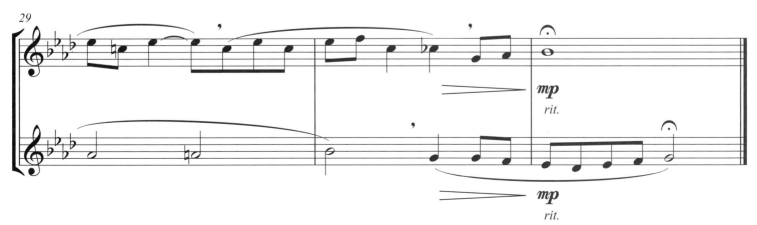

18. Not a Blues

This slow swing is really easy to rush on, so pay close attention to keeping an "unrushed" relaxed feel throughout. As with all of these duets, be sure to play the dynamic levels as indicated.

Not a Blues

19. Move It

"Move It" is a samba in 2 with some mixed articulation in the first two bars. Be sure to emphasize these articulations in order to bring them out, especially in bars 2, 5, and 6. There are no real difficult rhythms here, so try to play this up to tempo. Once again, any passages that give you a problem, play slowly, and gradually increase the tempo until you have achieved ♩ = 138.

Move It

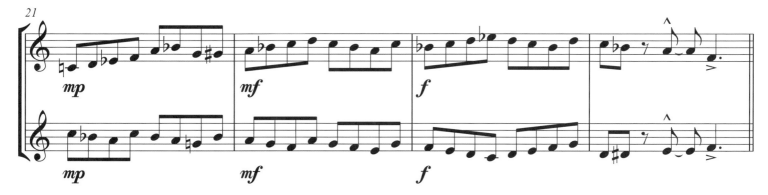

20. Nothing to See, Move Along

An easy swing that features lots of eighth-note triplets. Focus on *not rushing* through these triplet passages; try to keep it nice and relaxed. There are many instances where the eighth-note triplets are followed by eighth notes. Here is where it wants to rush, so just be aware of that.

Make sure your alignment of notes is accurate in bar 25. Starting at bar 21, it features some call and response between the two melodies; try to make that sound as "one" melody.

Nothing to See, Move Along

Easy Swing ♩ = 116

21. 3's Are Wild

Another situation where we have eighth notes phrased in groups of three. Watch out in the last bar as the phrasing changes. Once again, emphasize the accents.

3's Are Wild

Jazz Waltz ♩ = 160

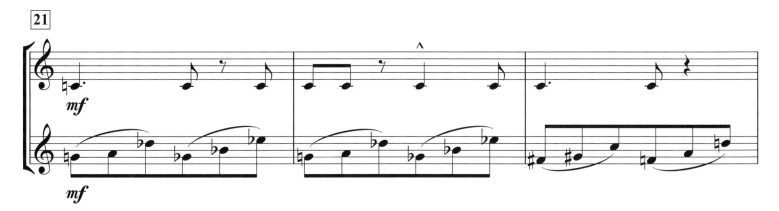

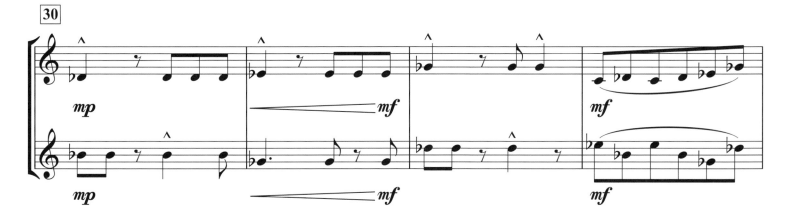

22. Symmetry

This duet is made up from two different scales. These scales are shared between the two parts.

Symmetric Diminished   **Whole Tone**

FIG. 22.1. C Symmetric Diminished and Whole Tone Scales

This may sound strange to you when both melodies are played together, but try to get the sound of your melody and the scale it is derived from in your ear. The challenge in playing this duet, is to play the intervals found within your scale, as accurately as possible. There are no particularly difficult passages in this duet. Just get used to the sound of your individual scale and the melodies it generates.

Symmetry

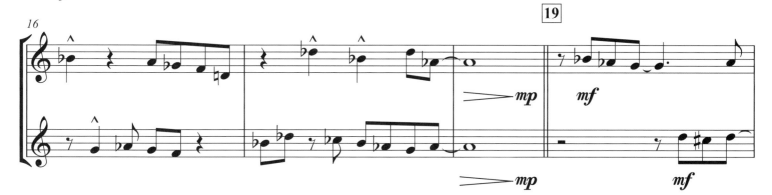

23. Salted Dominants

Both of these melodies are derived from an altered dominant scale. Once again, try
to get the sound of the scale in your ear.

Altered Dominant Scale

FIG. 23.1. C Altered Dominant Scale

All of the tied eighth notes are to be played long. The phrasing for this duet is
mostly four-bar phrases. As always, observe all dynamic markings.

Salted Dominants

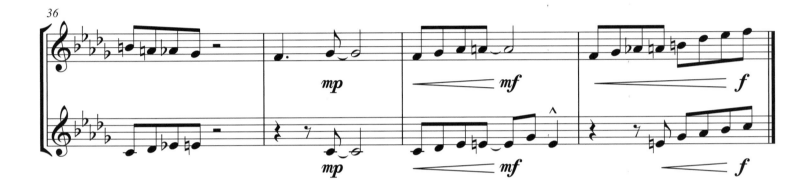

24. Hola

This samba in 2 has a lot of jazz staccato markings, so be sure to play them as short and "fat" as possible. Be aware of the mixed articulation in bar 15 and 28. Three bars from the end, there are some really important accents in both parts. Emphasize these accents. You will notice that each melody has its own placement of accents. When played together, and emphasized, there will be a composite rhythm that is a result of the different accents between lines.

Hola

Samba in 2 ♩ = 138

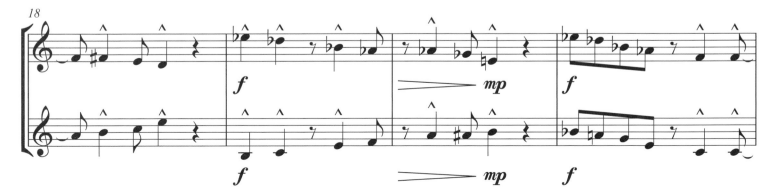

25. Pine Face Samba

If you're not in the habit of counting in 2, then this will be good practice for you. All sambas should be felt in 2, in order to get the proper feel. Rehearsal 23 has the second line entering on the "and" of 2, so counting in 2, your first note will be when your foot is up, and the next four eighth notes will be on the downbeat.

Pine Face Samba

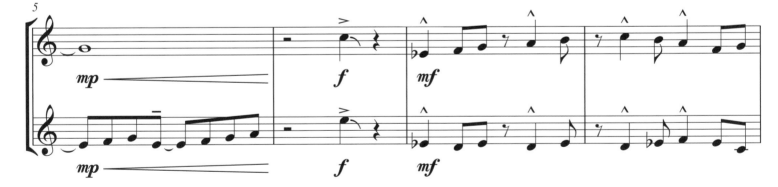

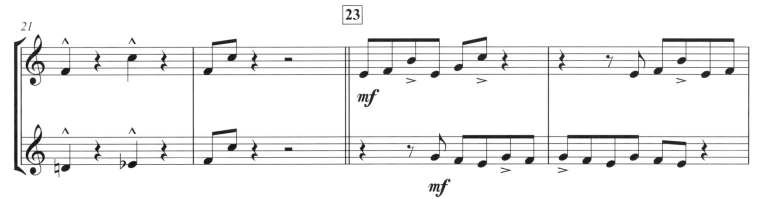

26. Bopishly

This duet features some angular melodies, so getting the sound of the intervals in your ear is important. The intervals in bar 18 and again at rehearsal 28 are difficult to hear, especially the second and third notes: the C♯ down to the C♮. Obviously, it becomes more difficult as the tempo increases. Just slowly play those two notes until you are comfortable with the sound of that interval.

Bopishly

Swing ♩ = 178

27. Pursuit

A fast swing piece where all of the tied eighths across the bar are to be played long. Realize once again that each line is its own melody and should be played as though it were the primary melody, rather than a secondary melody. I suggest you play this initially at a slower tempo and gradually work it up to the designated tempo.

Pursuit

Swing ♩ = 176

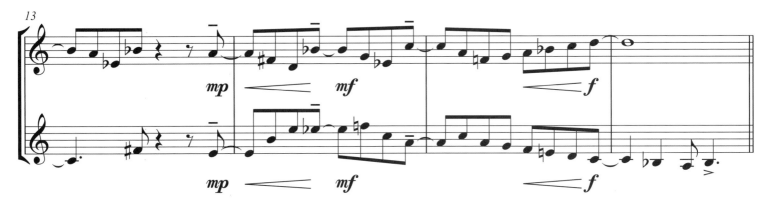

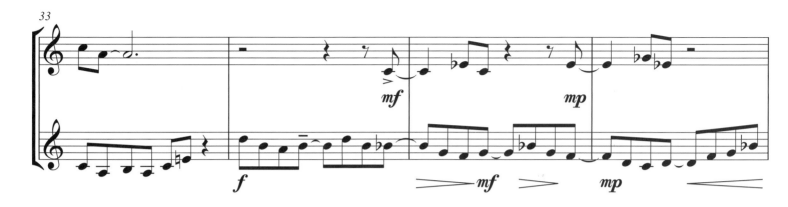

AFTERWORD

I would encourage you to try some of these duets at faster or slower tempos. The metronome markings I have included seem to fit the styles but you can certainly try different tempos. These duets can be played by any combination of instruments that play in the same key and share the same clef, and of course there can be more than one instrument on any of the lines. Feel free to combine any of these that are close to the same metronome markings and create an extended piece. For example: "Not a Blues" and "Green Leapers" could be combined, with the last measure of "Not a Blues" continuing into the first bar of "Green Leapers." You could also do the opposite, with the last bar of "Green Leapers" continuing on into the first bar of "Not a Blues."

The two sambas, "Pine Face Samba" and "Hola," could be combined by leaving a measure of rest between the end of either and continuing on to the next.

"Shake & Bake" and "Big Skippy" could also be combined, going from the last measure of "Shake & Bake" into the first measure of "Big Skippy."

Above all else, please have fun with these duets. I hope you enjoy them.

ABOUT THE AUTHOR

Richard Lowell is a trumpet player, composer, arranger, and educator. After a stint in the army where he played with the 19th Army Band, he joined the faculty of Berklee College of Music, where he trained thousands of musicians, over nearly five decades.

As a trumpet player, he performed with Tony Bennett, Lou Rawls, Steve Lawrence & Eydie Gorme, Mel Torme, Paul Anka, Johnny Mathis, Jack Jones, *The Steve Allen Show*, Ray Charles, Sammy Davis Jr., Dionne Warwick, Burt Bacharach, and many others. As an arranger and composer, he is credited on recordings by the Dave Stahl Big Band, Bombay Jim and the Swinging Sapphires, Dick Johnson, Ida Zecco, Jim Porcells (featured on the HBO series *Family Bonds*), the Kenny Hadley Big Band, and several works for a variety of educational institutions. He is co-author (with Ken Pullig) of *Arranging for Large Jazz Ensemble* (Berklee Press, 2003).

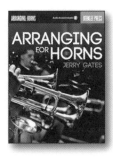

Berklee Press

Your Source for Composing, Arranging & Conducting

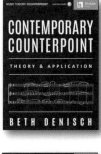

ARRANGING FOR HORNS
by Jerry Gates
00121625 Book/Online Audio $19.99

ARRANGING FOR LARGE JAZZ ENSEMBLE
by Dick Lowell and Ken Pullig
50449528 Book/Online Audio $39.99

ARRANGING FOR STRINGS
by Mimi Rabson
00190207 Book/Online Audio $19.99

THE BERKLEE BOOK OF JAZZ HARMONY
by Joe Mulholland & Tom Hojnacki
00113755 Book/Online Audio $27.50

BERKLEE CONTEMPORARY MUSIC NOTATION
by Jonathan Feist
00202547 Book $19.99

BERKLEE MUSIC THEORY
by Paul Schmeling
Book 1: Basic Principles of Rhythm, Scales and Intervals
50449615 Book/Online Audio $24.99
Book 2:
50449616 Book/Online Audio $22.99

COMPLETE GUIDE TO FILM SCORING
The Art and Business of Writing Music for Movies and TV
by Richard Davis
50449607 Book $29.99

CONDUCTING MUSIC TODAY
by Bruce Hangen
00237719 Book/Online Video....................$24.99

CONTEMPORARY COUNTERPOINT
Theory & Application
by Beth Denisch
00147050 Book/Online Audio $22.99

COUNTERPOINT IN JAZZ ARRANGING
by Bob Pilkington
00294301 Book/Online Audio $24.99

CREATING COMMERCIAL MUSIC
Advertising • Library Music • TV Themes
by Peter Bell
00278535 Book/Online Media....................$19.99

CREATIVE STRATEGIES IN FILM SCORING
by Ben Newhouse
00242911 Book/Online Media....................$24.99

JAZZ COMPOSITION
Theory and Practice
by Ted Pease
50448000 Book/Online Audio $39.99

JAZZ EXPRESSION
A Toolbox for Improvisation
with Larry Monroe
50448036 DVD....................................$19.95

MODERN JAZZ VOICINGS
Arranging for Small and Medium Ensembles
by Ted Pease and Ken Pullig
50449485 Book/Online Audio $24.99

MUSIC COMPOSITION FOR FILM AND TELEVISION
by Lalo Schifrin
50449604 Book $34.99

MUSIC NOTATION
Theory & Technique for Music Notation
by Mark McGrain
50449399 Book $24.99

MUSIC NOTATION
Preparing Scores and Parts
by Matthew Nicholl and Richard Grudzinski
50449540 Book $19.99

REHARMONIZATION TECHNIQUES
by Randy Felts
50449496 Book $29.99

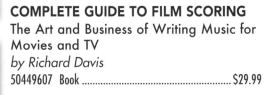

Berklee Press publications feature material developed at Berklee College of Music.

Visit your local music dealer or bookstore to order, or go to **www.berkleepress.com**

Prices, contents, and availability subject to change without notice.

More Fine Publications

Berklee Press

GUITAR

BEBOP GUITAR SOLOS
by Michael Kaplan
00121703 Book $16.99

BLUES GUITAR TECHNIQUE
by Michael Williams
50449623 Book/Online Audio...........$24.99

BERKLEE GUITAR CHORD DICTIONARY
by Rick Peckham
50449546 Jazz – Book..........................$12.99
50449596 Rock – Book.........................$12.99

BERKLEE GUITAR STYLE STUDIES
by Jim Kelly
00200377 Book/Online Media...........$24.99

CLASSICAL TECHNIQUE FOR THE MODERN GUITARIST
by Kim Perlak
00148781 Book/Online Audio..............$19.99

CONTEMPORARY JAZZ GUITAR SOLOS
by Michael Kaplan
00143596 Book...$16.99

CREATIVE CHORDAL HARMONY FOR GUITAR
by Mick Goodrick and Tim Miller
50449613 Book/Online Audio.............$19.99

FUNK/R&B GUITAR
by Thaddeus Hogarth
50449569 Book/Online Audio............$19.99

GUITAR SWEEP PICKING
by Joe Stump
00151223 Book/Online Audio..............$19.99

INTRODUCTION TO JAZZ GUITAR
by Jane Miller
00125041 Book/Online Audio..............$19.99

JAZZ GUITAR FRETBOARD NAVIGATION
by Mark White
00154107 Book/Online Audio..............$19.99

JAZZ SWING GUITAR
by Jon Wheatley
00139935 Book/Online Audio.............$19.99

METAL GUITAR CHOP SHOP
by Joe Stump
50449601 Book/Online Audio $19.99

A MODERN METHOD FOR GUITAR – VOLUMES 1-3 COMPLETE*
by William Leavitt
00292990 Book/Online Media $49.99
*Individual volumes, media options, and supporting songbooks available.

A MODERN METHOD FOR GUITAR SCALES
by Larry Baione
00199318 Book..................................$10.99

READING STUDIES FOR GUITAR
by William Leavitt
50449490 Book...$16.99

Berklee Press publications feature material developed at Berklee College of Music. To browse the complete Berklee Press Catalog, go to
www.berkleepress.com

BASS

BERKLEE JAZZ BASS
by Rich Appleman, Whit Browne & Bruce Gertz
50449636 Book/Online Audio............$19.99

CHORD STUDIES FOR ELECTRIC BASS
by Rich Appleman & Joseph Viola
50449750 Book $17.99

FINGERSTYLE FUNK BASS LINES
by Joe Santerre
50449542 Book/Online Audio...........$19.99

FUNK BASS FILLS
by Anthony Vitti
50449608 Book/Online Audio $19.99

INSTANT BASS
by Danny Morris
50449502 Book/CD.................................$9.99

METAL BASS LINES
by David Marvuglio
00122465 Book/Online Audio.............$19.99

READING CONTEMPORARY ELECTRIC BASS
by Rich Appleman
50449770 Book $19.99

ROCK BASS LINES
by Joe Santerre
50449478 Book/Online Audio...........$22.99

PIANO/KEYBOARD

BERKLEE JAZZ KEYBOARD HARMONY
by Suzanna Sifter
00138874 Book/Online Audio $24.99

BERKLEE JAZZ PIANO
by Ray Santisi
50448047 Book/Online Audio $19.99

BERKLEE JAZZ STANDARDS FOR SOLO PIANO
arr. Robert Christopherson, Hey Rim Jeon, Ross Ramsay, Tim Ray
00160482 Book/Online Audio $19.99

CHORD-SCALE IMPROVISATION FOR KEYBOARD
by Ross Ramsay
50449597 Book/CD $19.99

CONTEMPORARY PIANO TECHNIQUE
by Stephany Tiernan
50449545 Book/DVD.........................$29.99

HAMMOND ORGAN COMPLETE
by Dave Limina
00237801 Book/Online Audio...........$24.99

JAZZ PIANO COMPING
by Suzanne Davis
50449614 Book/Online Audio.............$19.99

LATIN JAZZ PIANO IMPROVISATION
by Rebecca Cline
50449649 Book/Online Audio $24.99

PIANO ESSENTIALS
by Ross Ramsay
50448046 Book/Online Audio $24.99

SOLO JAZZ PIANO
by Neil Olmstead
50449641 Book/Online Audio...........$39.99

DRUMS

BEGINNING DJEMBE
by Michael Markus & Joe Galeota
00148210 Book/Online Video.............$16.99

BERKLEE JAZZ DRUMS
by Casey Scheuerell
50449612 Book/Online Audio.............$19.99

DRUM SET WARM-UPS
by Rod Morgenstein
50449465 Book.....................................$12.99

A MANUAL FOR THE MODERN DRUMMER
by Alan Dawson & Don DeMichael
50449560 Book.......................................$14.99

MASTERING THE ART OF BRUSHES
by Jon Hazilla
50449459 Book/Online Audio............$19.99

PHRASING
by Russ Gold
00120209 Book/Online Media $19.99

WORLD JAZZ DRUMMING
by Mark Walker
50449568 Book/CD $22.99

BERKLEE PRACTICE METHOD

GET YOUR BAND TOGETHER
With additional volumes for other instruments, plus a teacher's guide.
Bass
by Rich Appleman, John Repucci and the Berklee Faculty
50449427 Book/CD $19.99
Drum Set
by Ron Savage, Casey Scheuerell and the Berklee Faculty
50449429 Book/CD.................................$14.95
Guitar
by Larry Baione and the Berklee Faculty
50449426 Book/CD.................................$19.99
Keyboard
by Russell Hoffmann, Paul Schmeling and the Berklee Faculty
50449428 Book/Online Audio............$14.99

VOICE

BELTING
by Jeannie Gagné
00124984 Book/Online Media.............$19.99

THE CONTEMPORARY SINGER
by Anne Peckham
50449595 Book/Online Audio...........$24.99

JAZZ VOCAL IMPROVISATION
by Mili Bermejo
00159290 Book/Online Audio.............$19.99

TIPS FOR SINGERS
by Carolyn Wilkins
50449557 Book/CD $19.95

VOCAL WORKOUTS FOR THE CONTEMPORARY SINGER
by Anne Peckham
50448044 Book/Online Audio..........$24.99

YOUR SINGING VOICE
by Jeannie Gagné
50449619 Book/Online Audio..........$29.99

WOODWINDS & BRASS

TRUMPET SOUND EFFECTS
by Craig Pederson & Ueli Dörig
00121626 Book/Online Audio............$14.99

SAXOPHONE SOUND EFFECTS
by Ueli Dörig
50449628 Book/Online Audio..........$15.99

THE TECHNIQUE OF THE FLUTE
by Joseph Viola
00214012 Book.............................$19.99

STRINGS/ROOTS MUSIC

BERKLEE HARP
by Felice Pomeranz
00144263 Book/Online Audio............$19.99

BEYOND BLUEGRASS BANJO
by Dave Hollander and Matt Glaser
50449610 Book/CD.............................$19.99

BEYOND BLUEGRASS MANDOLIN
by John McGann and Matt Glaser
50449609 Book/CD.............................$19.99

BLUEGRASS FIDDLE & BEYOND
by Matt Glaser
50449602 Book/CD.............................$19.99

CONTEMPORARY CELLO ETUDES
by Mike Block
00159292 Book/Online Audio............$19.99

EXPLORING CLASSICAL MANDOLIN
by August Watters
00125040 Book/Online Media..........$22.99

THE IRISH CELLO BOOK
by Liz Davis Maxfield
50449652 Book/Online Audio..........$24.99

JAZZ UKULELE
by Abe Lagrimas, Jr.
00121624 Book/Online Audio............$19.99

WELLNESS

MANAGE YOUR STRESS AND PAIN THROUGH MUSIC
by Dr. Suzanne B. Hanser and Dr. Susan E. Mandel
50449592 Book/CD $29.99

MUSICIAN'S YOGA
by Mia Olson
50449587 Book.............................$19.99

NEW MUSIC THERAPIST'S HANDBOOK
by Dr. Suzanne B. Hanser
00279325 Book.............................$29.99

MUSIC PRODUCTION & ENGINEERING

AUDIO MASTERING
by Jonathan Wyner
50449581 Book/CD $29.99

AUDIO POST PRODUCTION
by Mark Cross
50449627 Book.............................$19.99

CREATING COMMERCIAL MUSIC
by Peter Bell
00278535 Book/Online Media $19.99

THE SINGER-SONGWRITER'S GUIDE TO RECORDING IN THE HOME STUDIO
by Shane Adams
00148211 Book.............................$16.99

UNDERSTANDING AUDIO
by Daniel M. Thompson
00148197 Book.............................$34.99

MUSIC BUSINESS

CROWDFUNDING FOR MUSICIANS
by Laser Malena-Webber
00285092 Book.............................$17.99

ENGAGING THE CONCERT AUDIENCE
by David Wallace
00244532 Book/Online Media..........$16.99

HOW TO GET A JOB IN THE MUSIC INDUSTRY
by Keith Hatschek with Breanne Beseda
00130699 Book.............................$27.99

MAKING MUSIC MAKE MONEY
by Eric Beall
50448009 Book.............................$29.99

MUSIC INDUSTRY FORMS
by Jonathan Feist
00121814 Book.............................$15.99

MUSIC LAW IN THE DIGITAL AGE
by Allen Bargfrede
00148196 Book.............................$19.99

MUSIC MARKETING
by Mike King
50449588 Book.............................$24.99

PROJECT MANAGEMENT FOR MUSICIANS
by Jonathan Feist
50449659 Book.............................$29.99

THE SELF-PROMOTING MUSICIAN
by Peter Spellman
00119607 Book.............................$24.99

CONDUCTING

CONDUCTING MUSIC TODAY
by Bruce Hangen
00237719 Book/Online Media..........$24.99

MUSIC THEORY & EAR TRAINING

BEGINNING EAR TRAINING
by Gilson Schachnik
50449548 Book/Online Audio..........$16.99

BERKLEE CONTEMPORARY MUSIC NOTATION
by Jonathan Feist
00202547 Book.............................$19.99

BERKLEE MUSIC THEORY
by Paul Schmeling
50449615 Book 1/Online Audio........$24.99
50449616 Book 2/Online Audio.......$22.99

CONTEMPORARY COUNTERPOINT
by Beth Denisch
00147050 Book/Online Audio..........$22.99

MUSIC NOTATION
by Mark McGrain
50449399 Book.............................$24.99
by Matthew Nicholl & Richard Grudzinski
50449540 Book.............................$19.99

REHARMONIZATION TECHNIQUES
by Randy Felts
50449496 Book.............................$29.99

SONGWRITING/COMPOSING

BEGINNING SONGWRITING
by Andrea Stolpe with Jan Stolpe
00138503 Book/Online Audio...........$19.99

COMPLETE GUIDE TO FILM SCORING
by Richard Davis
50449607 Book.............................$29.99

THE CRAFT OF SONGWRITING
by Scarlet Keys
00159283 Book/Online Audio...........$19.99

CREATIVE STRATEGIES IN FILM SCORING
by Ben Newhouse
00242911 Book/Online Media...........$24.99

JAZZ COMPOSITION
by Ted Pease
50448000 Book/Online Audio $39.99

MELODY IN SONGWRITING
by Jack Perricone
50449419 Book.............................$24.99

MUSIC COMPOSITION FOR FILM AND TELEVISION
by Lalo Schifrin
50449604 Book.............................$34.99

POPULAR LYRIC WRITING
by Andrea Stolpe
50449553 Book.............................$15.99

THE SONGWRITER'S WORKSHOP
by Jimmy Kachulis
Harmony
50449519 Book/Online Audio $29.99
Melody
50449518 Book/Online Audio $24.99

SONGWRITING: ESSENTIAL GUIDE
by Pat Pattison
Lyric Form and Structure
50481582 Book.............................$16.99
Rhyming
00124366 Book.............................$17.99

SONGWRITING IN PRACTICE
by Mark Simos
00244545 Book.............................$16.99

SONGWRITING STRATEGIES
by Mark Simos
50449621 Book.............................$24.99

ARRANGING & IMPROVISATION

ARRANGING FOR HORNS
by Jerry Gates
00121625 Book/Online Audio............$19.99

BERKLEE BOOK OF JAZZ HARMONY
by Joe Mulholland & Tom Hojnacki
00113755 Book/Online Audio $27.50

IMPROVISATION FOR CLASSICAL MUSICIANS
by Eugene Friesen with Wendy M. Friesen
50449637 Book/CD $24.99

MODERN JAZZ VOICINGS
by Ted Pease and Ken Pullig
50449485 Book/Online Audio..........$24.99

AUTOBIOGRAPHY

LEARNING TO LISTEN: THE JAZZ JOURNEY OF GARY BURTON
by Gary Burton
00117798 Book.............................$27.99

Prices subject to change without notice. Visit your local music dealer or bookstore, or go to **www.berkleepress.com**